COUNTRIES

RUSSIA

by Cynthia Kennedy Henzel

FOCUS READERS®
NAVIGATOR

WWW.FOCUSREADERS.COM

Copyright © 2025 by Focus Readers®, Mendota Heights, MN 55120. All rights reserved. No part of this book may be reproduced or utilized in any form or by any means without written permission from the publisher.

Focus Readers is distributed by North Star Editions:
sales@northstareditions.com | 888-417-0195

Produced for Focus Readers by Red Line Editorial.

Content Consultant: Natalya Peretyatko, Adjunct Lecturer of Russian Studies, College of William & Mary

Photographs ©: Shutterstock Images, cover, 1, 4–5, 7, 14–15, 17, 19, 20–21, 23, 24, 26–27; iStockphoto, 8–9; The Print Collector/Hulton Archive/Getty Images, 11; Bettmann/Getty Images, 12; Linda Vartoogian/Archive Photos/Getty Images, 28

Library of Congress Cataloging-in-Publication Data
Names: Henzel, Cynthia Kennedy, 1954- author.
Title: Russia / by Cynthia Kennedy Henzel.
Description: Mendota Heights, MN: Focus Readers, 2025. | Series: Countries
    | Includes index. | Audience: Grades 4-6
Identifiers: LCCN 2024029263 (print) | LCCN 2024029264 (ebook) | ISBN
    9798889982265 (hardcover) | ISBN 9798889982821 (paperback) | ISBN
    9798889983880 (pdf) | ISBN 9798889983385 (ebook)
Subjects: LCSH: Russia (Federation)--Juvenile literature.
Classification: LCC DK510.23 .H469 2025 (print) | LCC DK510.23 (ebook) |
    DDC 947--dc23/eng/20240724
LC record available at https://lccn.loc.gov/2024029263
LC ebook record available at https://lccn.loc.gov/2024029264

Printed in the United States of America
Mankato, MN
012025

ABOUT THE AUTHOR
Cynthia Kennedy Henzel has a BS in social studies education and an MS in geography. She has worked as a teacher-educator in many countries. Currently, she writes fiction and nonfiction books and develops education materials for social studies, history, science, and ELL students. She has written more than 100 books and more than 150 stories for young people.

TABLE OF CONTENTS

CHAPTER 1
Welcome to Russia 5

CHAPTER 2
History 9

CHAPTER 3
Climate, Plants, and Animals 15

CLIMATE CRISIS IN RUSSIA
Losing Land 18

CHAPTER 4
Resources, Economy, and Government 21

CHAPTER 5
People and Culture 27

Focus Questions • 30
Glossary • 31
To Learn More • 32
Index • 32

CHAPTER 1

WELCOME TO RUSSIA

Russia is the world's largest country. It covers approximately one-tenth of all land on Earth. Russia is part of two different continents. The area west of the Ural Mountains is in Europe. The land to the east is in Asia.

Most of Russia's large cities are in the European part. Moscow is Russia's capital

More than 12 million people live in Moscow, Russia.

5

and biggest city. The second-largest city is St. Petersburg. It is a major seaport. From there, many ships sail the Baltic Sea. They carry oil and other products from the country's factories, which are mostly in western Russia.

   Much of western Russian has low hills or plains. The Volga River is also in western Russia. It is the longest river in Europe. The Volga flows south to the Caspian Sea. The Caspian Sea is the largest saltwater lake in the world. Russia borders the Black Sea in the southwest.

   East of the Ural Mountains is Siberia. This vast, cold area covers approximately three-fourths of Russia's land. But only one-fourth of the country's population lives there. Great rivers flow north to the Arctic Ocean. In the south is Lake Baikal. It contains more fresh water than any other lake on Earth.

MAP OF RUSSIA

CHAPTER 2

HISTORY

Small tribes lived in Russia as early as 40,000 years ago. In the 800s CE, foreign traders began taking over. Some came from Scandinavia. They formed a state called Kyivan Rus. Others invaded from the east. For example, the Mongols took over in the 1200s. They ruled until the mid-1400s. Then several Rus princes

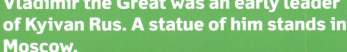

Vladimir the Great was an early leader of Kyivan Rus. A statue of him stands in Moscow.

defeated them. The princes formed a new state. Its capital was in Moscow.

In 1547, Ivan IV became the first tsar, or leader of all Russia. Later tsars added even more land. They took over parts of Siberia and eastern Europe. By the end of the 1600s, Russia was a large country. A family called the Romanovs ruled it. Some leaders, such as Peter the Great, made big changes. But the tsars' strict rule sometimes sparked unrest.

Russia kept adding land in the 1800s and 1900s. However, unrest also grew. Common people wanted more power. Groups such as the Bolsheviks called for change. Vladimir Lenin led the

The Romanov family ruled Russia from 1613 to 1917. Nicholas II (second from left) was the last tsar.

Bolsheviks. They took over Russia's government in 1917. A civil war broke out.

In 1922, the Soviet Union formed. It was a group of 15 **Communist** states. Russia was one of them. Joseph Stalin became the Soviet Union's leader in 1924. He was a harsh **dictator**. He killed or jailed his enemies. Under Stalin,

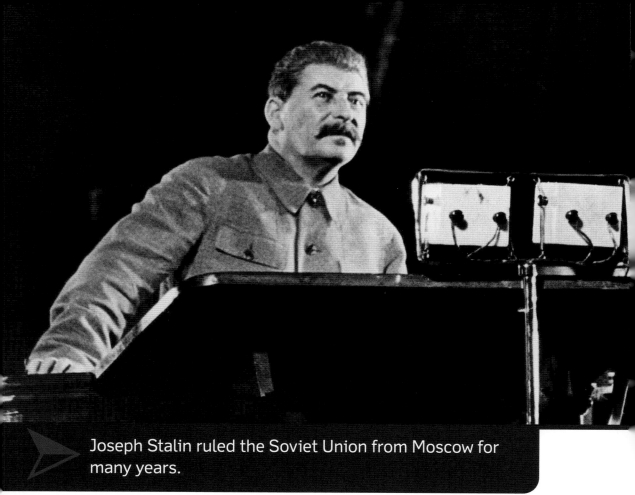

Joseph Stalin ruled the Soviet Union from Moscow for many years.

the Soviet government seized farms and factories. Food ran out. Millions of people died.

The Soviet Union helped the **Allies** win World War II (1939–1945). Afterward, it grew powerful. It developed **nuclear**

weapons. And it tried to get other countries to become Communist. This caused tension with Western countries, including the United States. The strain was known as the Cold War.

Stalin died in 1953. Later leaders were more open to Western ideas. By the 1970s, the Soviet Union was struggling. In 1991, it split into 15 independent countries. One was Russia.

THE SPACE RACE

During the Cold War, the Soviet Union and the United States competed to explore space. In 1957, the Soviets put the first satellite into orbit around Earth. And in 1961, Yuri Gagarin became the first person in space. But the United States reached the moon first.

CHAPTER 3

CLIMATE, PLANTS, AND ANIMALS

Most of Russia is cold. Tundra stretches across the north. Tundra is so cold that a layer of soil, called permafrost, never thaws. As a result, hardly any trees grow there.

Summers in the tundra are short and cool. Little rain falls. But the ground stays wet in the cool air. Moss and **lichen** grow

Reindeer live in Russia's tundra.

in the top inches of thawed soil. They provide food for reindeer. Arctic foxes live in the tundra, too.

South of the tundra is the taiga. Many evergreen trees grow in this region. It has large forests of spruce and pine. Many animals make their homes among the trees. They include birds, elk, and bears.

SIBERIAN TIGER

Siberian tigers live in the taiga. These animals nearly died out. In the 1930s, fewer than 30 wild tigers remained. Today, there are several hundred. But the tigers are still endangered. People hunt them illegally. People also destroy the forests where the tigers live.

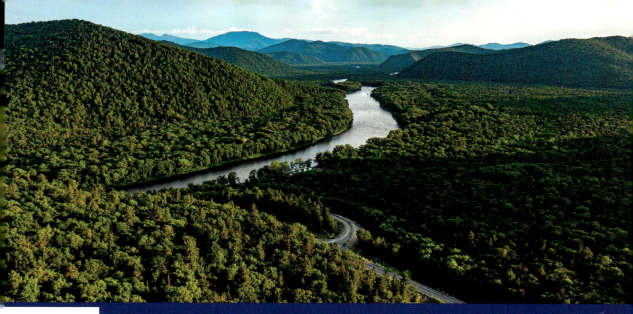

Russia has more than 100,000 rivers and one-fifth of the world's trees.

Further south are Russia's steppes. These large areas of grass are too dry for trees to grow. But wolves and wild horses live there.

Southwest Russia has a climate that is good for farming. This area has four seasons. Summers are hot and wet. Winters are cold. But the ground thaws again in spring.

CLIMATE CRISIS IN RUSSIA

LOSING LAND

Climate change is causing severe problems in Russia. One problem involves permafrost. Permafrost covers two-thirds of Russia. Rising temperatures are causing this layer to thaw. When that happens, the ground becomes less stable. It can shift or turn to mud. These changes damage roads and buildings.

More than two million Russians live in Arctic cities. Thawing is a threat to their homes. Russia also has miles of pipelines. They send oil and gas across the country. But unstable ground can cause pipelines to break. Melting permafrost also lets out greenhouse gases. These gases make climate change worse.

Climate change is bad for farming, too. It makes droughts more common. Crops such as wheat become harder to grow. Hotter weather and droughts also make wildfires more likely.

Yakutia is an area in Siberia. It contains Yakutsk, one of two big cities in Russia built on top of permafrost.

In the 2020s, fires have destroyed large parts of Russia's forests.

Fossil fuels are a major cause of climate change. Using more **sustainable** energy sources can lessen this impact. However, Russia sells lots of oil and gas. So, using less fuel would require big changes.

CHAPTER 4

RESOURCES, ECONOMY, AND GOVERNMENT

Russia has many natural resources. It produces one-fifth of the world's oil and one-fourth of the world's natural gas. It's also a major source of metal and coal. Vast forests are another key resource. They cover nearly two-thirds of the country. They supply wood and paper.

Russia has more natural gas reserves than any other country.

Fishing is important near coasts. The Caspian Sea is famous for its sturgeon. The fish's eggs are called black caviar. This expensive food is a major **export**.

Russia's plains are known for growing grain. Big companies often run large farms. Wheat is the most common crop.

Most Russians live in cities. Many people work in services, such as banking or transportation. Because Russia is so big, moving goods can be difficult. Railroads help. Other Russians work in factories. Many build machines or vehicles. Others process chemicals or oil.

Russia has a strong central government. People vote to elect a

Sheep and cattle graze on grasses on Russia's steppes.

president. This leader then appoints ministers. Russia also has a legislature. This group makes the country's laws. However, the president has power over the legislature. He can call new elections. And he can change laws.

Vladimir Putin has led Russia's government since 1999. He has worked

Russia's government is based in a building called the Kremlin.

to expand its power. In 2014, Russia took over Crimea. That area had been part of Ukraine. Russian troops invaded Ukraine in 2022. They expected an easy win. But Ukrainians fought back. War continued for several years.

Many countries condemned Russia's actions in Ukraine. Some gave aid to

Ukraine. Some put **sanctions** on Russia. These bans made it harder for Russia to make money. Putin was also charged with war crimes. His actions within Russia have raised concern as well. His government tightly controls information. And his opponents often end up in jail or even dead.

SUSPICIOUS CRASH

Yevgeny Prigozhin led a private army called the Wagner Group. This army helped Russia invade Ukraine in 2022. At first, Putin and Prigozhin were friends. But in June 2023, Prigozhin told his troops to march to Moscow. He called them back before they reached the capital. But Putin said he was a traitor. Two months later, Prigozhin died in a plane crash.

CHAPTER 5

PEOPLE AND CULTURE

As of 2024, Russia was home to 144 million people. Many were Russian. But the country has more than 120 ethnic groups. These include Tatars, Chechens, and Ukrainians. Each group brings its own foods, language, and traditions.

Christianity is Russia's most common religion. For many years, tsars formed

Russian churches often display icons. These images are important to both art and religion.

Swan Lake is a famous ballet. A Russian composer named Pyotr Ilyich Tchaikovsky wrote it.

official ties to the Russian Orthodox church. But Muslims and Jews also have long histories in Russia. And 26 percent of Russians don't identify with any faith.

Russia is famous for art and music, especially ballet. It has produced many composers, dancers, and theaters. It has also shaped several styles of painting and **architecture**. Russian writers are influential, too. They include Fyodor Dostoyevsky and Leo Tolstoy. People around the world study their work.

Russia also produces top athletes. They win many international events. For example, its gymnasts and figure skaters have earned many Olympic medals.

ARTISTS RESIST

Russia's government has often controlled much of the country's media. Books, TV, and radio were censored under the Soviet government. Today, Russia's government runs many TV stations. It even limits what people see online. Criticizing leaders is risky. But some artists still do it. They stand up for what they believe in.

FOCUS QUESTIONS

Write your answers on a separate piece of paper.

1. Write a paragraph describing some of Russia's important natural resources.

2. Would you rather visit Russia's tundra, taiga, or steppes? Why?

3. Who was the leader of the Bolsheviks?
    - **A.** Vladimir Lenin
    - **B.** Ivan IV
    - **C.** Vladimir Putin

4. How could sanctions cause a government to stop doing something?
    - **A.** The government could want the sanctions to keep going.
    - **B.** The government could want the sanctions to end.
    - **C.** The sanctions could give the government more money.

Answer key on page 32.

GLOSSARY

Allies
The group of countries that won World War II.

architecture
The art of designing and constructing buildings.

climate change
A human-caused global crisis involving long-term changes in Earth's temperature and weather patterns.

Communist
Belonging to a political system in which all property is owned by the government.

dictator
A leader with absolute power.

export
Something that is sent to other countries for sale.

lichen
A plant-like living thing made of algae and fungus.

nuclear weapons
Bombs or missiles that create huge explosions by splitting atoms.

sanctions
Penalties meant to force a country to change its behavior.

sustainable
Using methods that do not harm or use up a resource.

TO LEARN MORE

BOOKS
Marshall, Deb. *Russia*. New York: AV2, 2022.
Van, R. L. *Russia*. Minneapolis: Abdo Publishing, 2023.
Walker, Tracy Sue. *Spotlight on Russia*. Minneapolis: Lerner Publications, 2024.

NOTE TO EDUCATORS
Visit **www.focusreaders.com** to find lesson plans, activities, links, and other resources related to this title.

INDEX

art, 28–29
athletes, 29

Bolsheviks, 10–11

Caspian Sea, 6–7, 22
climate change, 18–19
Cold War, 13

Kyivan Rus, 9

Lake Baikal, 7

Lenin, Vladimir, 10

Moscow, 5, 7, 10, 25

permafrost, 15, 18
Putin, Vladimir, 23, 25

Siberia, 6–7, 10
Soviet Union, 11–13, 29
Stalin, Joseph, 11, 13
steppes, 17

St. Petersburg, 6–7

taiga, 16
tsars, 10, 27
tundra, 15–16

Ukraine, 7, 24–25
Ural Mountains, 5–7

Volga River, 6–7

Answer Key: 1. Answers will vary; 2. Answers will vary; 3. A; 4. B